Skinny Writing

Skinny Writing

A Guide
To Concise Prose
for Writers and Editors

by Dick Heaberlin

Writing Style 4

Orange House Books

San Marcos, Texas

For additional information visit the author's website at
dickheaberlinwrites.com

ISBN 978-0-9794964-2-4

About This Book

I have written this book to save time—mine in not having to repeat its information to each student and each class and that of readers of my students' prose. This book is about clear and economical writing. In it I provide detailed explanations of ways to eliminate redundant words and phrases. I have used this information in lectures and conferences since 1959 when I taught writing to seventh graders in Dickinson Junior High School, just south of Houston. After that I taught writing to tenth graders in Irving, then to college freshmen at Tarleton State College, and to all levels of students at Texas State University. I employed the same strategies in co-editing two academic journals, *Southwest American Literature* from 1992 until 2012 and *Texas Books in Review* from 1995 until 2012.

This book is the fourth in my series of *Guides to Writing Style*. Its readers do not need to have studied the other guides to understand its information, but a knowledge of English syntax is useful whenever studying writing. All level of writers can benefit from using the techniques and information gained from the explanations and exercises.

Contents

Lesson 1

Repetition and Redundancy

Skillful writers often use repetition effectively, choosing to repeat a word or concept to emphasize it or to clarify connections. For emphasis, those writers may choose an appositive, a kind of repetition. They may write, "I bought a new car, a car with great economy and great power." The second use of *car* is the appositive. They also used *great* twice for emphasis when they could have said the same thing by omitting the second *great*. They may often use pronouns repeatedly to show that the same agent is acting in several sentences—to make clear connection between sentences. Notice that I have used *they* to connect several of the previous sentences.

I treat skillful repetition in some detail in my guidebook *Connecting for Coherence*. The kind of repetition many readers hate is often called redundancy. If you read this guidebook and do the exercises, you will learn how to avoid many common kinds of ineffective repetition and thus make your readers happy.

We call the use of excess words by several names—*redundancies, pleonasms, tautologies*. According to the *Oxford English Dictionary*, none of these words were found in written English before 1572, well into the Early Modern English period. The first written use in English of words for this concept was of *redundance*. The *OED* reports this translation from Latin: "Origene tooke great paynes to correct the seauentie Translators, adding of his owne where he thought they were not full, and taking from them where he sawe redundance and superfluitie." The *OED* reports *redundancy* in 1601: "There is in them me thinketh great redundancie of wordes, which might wel be spared." *Pleonasm* is first cited in 1610, but the second citation, from Burton's *Melancholy*, is more interesting: "I require a fauourable censure of all faults omitted, harsh compositions, pleonasmes of words, Tautologicall repetitions,.&c." The word *Tautology* was first published in English in 1587, but two later citations are more relevant here: "To shew that there is no tautology, no vain repetition of one and the same thing therein." (1653) and "The Taedium of Tautology is odious to every Pen and Ear" (1687). So my goal here is to help you avoid "vain repetition" and avoid being odious.

The *Oxford English Dictionary* is a wonderful source of information about word origins, about etymology. In my class on the history of the English language, students learn about the many languages serving as sources for our lexicon, our word stock. The primary sources are the West Germanic languages, the words of the Angles, Saxons, and Jutes. During the time of the Viking raids on the English coast, many words of North Germanic origin came in, words from Danish, Swedish, and Norwegian. All of these languages are for the most part analytical. One important example of this is that most adverbs are separated from the verbs. So in modern times we may write that we will *come back, turn back, put something together, go forward, turn something away*.

But before and after the Norman conquest of England in 1066, words were borrowed into English from the Romance languages, mostly Latin and French. These languages are primarily synthetic. In these, most adverbial concepts are connected to the verbs. So today we may *progress, revert, divert, convert, compose*. The information carried by the prefix serves the same purpose as a separated adverb in the Germanic languages.

In hurried speech many of us will combine the two. We will say, "I'm going to combine the two together." Most listeners will not be bothered by the redundant *together,* which has the same meaning as the *com-* of combine. But readers are likely to be much less tolerant. Readers abhor and find odious vain repetition. Readers expect writers to take pains with their work and not make them read unnecessary words.

Redundancies of this sort can be corrected in two ways. I can go Germanic and change *combine* to *put,* "I'm going to put the two together." Or I can go Latinate and leave out *together,* "I'm going to combine the two." The Germanic is usually more informal and less economical, the Latinate more formal and concise.

Similar to this kind of redundancy is one which repeats information conveyed by an earlier word. Good examples of this are "tall in height, yellow in color, added bonus, and armed gunman."

Another common kind of redundancy is of an absolute needing no modification being modified. *Empty* is an absolute. It needs no modification, but it is often modified, *completely empty.*

In Exercise 1 you can enjoy eliminating unnecessary words of all three types.

Exercise 1

In the following sentences, strike through the unnecessary modifier or change the Latinate word to a Germanic one.

1. The wine glass is completely empty.

2. Pam's dress is the exact same as Lynn's.

3. That is an extremely unique expression of distaste.

4. It is absolutely essential that he buy this book.

5. The fire ants completely annihilated our quail.

6. Carol has consciously chosen to omit this part of the story from the family history.

7. It was marred by the brutal violence of Manifest Destiny.

8. Anglos completely demolished the fort and set fire to the church.

9. Following the conclusion of the Mexican-American War in 1848, Mexico ceded control of California and New Mexico to the United States in 1849.

10. In *Stagecoach*, the deviations from Ernest Haycox's "The Stage to Lordsburg" were relatively small in scale.

11. Unlike the virtuous frontier hero, McCarthy's "child" is the complete opposite.

12. We made advanced reservations for dinner.

13. He is working on the basic fundamentals of tennis.

14. I blended together a peach and a plum.

15. For a brief moment I gave it careful scrutiny.

16. We collaborated together in order to classify the insects into groups.

17. Fred and I competed with each other until the final completion of the match.

18. We saw with our own eyes how he was behaving.

19. Fred Thompson was extradited back last week.

20. The product was introduced for the first time on television at the Super Bowl football game.

21. I liked McCarthy's fiction novel *The Crossing*.

22. There has not yet been an announcement from the Provost's office.

23. He wrote an autobiography of his own life.

24. His home run gave the Bobcats a 3-2 lead, which they never relinquished the rest of the way.

25. The Owls lost their last game, a series ender against Tulane, but won four of their previous five before that.

26. The Rangers game with the Diamondbacks was postponed to a later date.

27. When he raised his voice to a higher level, it wasn't as clear.

28. He equates the two together.

29. I could just hear my sister saying the exact same things as Jen did in Act I.

Lesson 2

Handling Addition Economically

When a writer puts a period at the end of one sentence and uses an uppercase letter to begin a second one, there is an understood *and* connecting the two sentences. Young writers in grammar school often have placed *and* before every sentence. This habit was probably responsible for teachers' prohibiting students from writing sentences beginning with *and*. The teachers probably assumed because of their students' youth that they lacked the judgment to know when and when not to use *and* to begin a sentence.

But older writers write similarly, placing words such as *and*, *further*, and *also* between sentences when they are unnecessary. *And* is a good coordinating conjunction to show the logic of addition between two statements and can be used to begin sentences. But it is not needed before the coordinating conjunction *so*. One of my students regularly writes *and* before *so*. He wrote, "He worked hard, and so he was promoted." Another likes to put *further* with his *and*s: "They left town, and further they moved to Alaska."

Both and *all* are often unnecessarily added to sentences with *they* or plural nouns: "The marshal and his deputy ~~both~~ have a responsibility to Hadleyville." and "The townspeople ~~all~~ deny Kane's appeal for help." *As well* is often tagged on to sentences redundantly: "The marshal and his deputy have a responsibility to Hadleyville ~~as well~~."

Often prepositional phrases are confusingly and needlessly used to replace *and*: "William Kane as well as Harvey Pell has a responsibility to Hadleyville." Notice the confusion with verb agreement caused by this means of adding. The form of the verb *has* seems odd and calls attention to itself. *Along with* and *in addition to* are frequently used and cause the same problem: "The marshall along with his deputy has a responsibility to Hadleyville," and "The marshall in addition to his deputy has a responsibility to Hadleyville." I recommend substituting *and* for these prepositions.

Another wordy way to show addition often used is *not only* with *but*. Some writers use this routinely rather than the simple *and* connective. Instead of writing "Bob and Mary went to see *Batman*," they write, "Not only Bob but also Mary went to see

Batman. "The *not-only-but* construction should be used only when the last one of the pair is a surprise. Conjunctive adverbs for addition often are overly formal—*moreover, furthermore, additionally*—or are too informal—*what's more* or *plus*. I like the ones which pull little focus, *too* and *also*. Often all of these are superfluous when addition is already clear.

Exercise 1

In the following sentences, strike through any unnecessary words for addition or rewrite the sentence to eliminate any redundancies.

1. His sense of self is discontinuous with the identity he has created in the rest of the family narrative, and so he has chosen not to tell the story until this moment.

2. It encouraged this sense of optimism as well as the demand for more territory.

3. He was tired not only of reading essays but also of writing themes.

4. Not only was he arrested, but he was additionally sent to prison, too.

5. Bill with his friend is going to be able to work during the holidays.

6. Tom and Bill both wanted to go to a college in the Southwest.

7. The pilgrims all suffered during that first winter.

8. Bill lost most of his money gambling. And what's more he had no way to get home.

9. Guy along with Ralph is leaving for Boston soon.

10. He ate three pieces of pie and some ice cream as well.

Exercise 2

In the following sentences, strike through the redundant words or rewrite the sentence to avoid the extra words. In some there will be more than one thing to remove.

1. Not only was Bill completely lost, but Gilbert was, too.

2. And, moreover, both their stories were incredible to believe.

3. They all joined together for a joint collaboration.

4. They both knelt down to be knighted.

5. Their past history was completely full of bad misbehavior as well.

6. They all will meet with each other to discuss a major breakthrough.

7. Not only have they together been responsible for new innovations but also for new inventions as well.

8. Not only were they all proud of what they had originally created, but they also over exaggerated its importance.

9. My past experience along with my past record shows how I have completely eliminated my bad misdeeds.

10. He further couldn't possibly descend down into the depths of sad depressive feelings without joining together with his friends to discuss his problem.

11. Additionally, the second half of this film also seems to drag on and on forever with scenes that do nothing to propel the storyline forward.

Lesson 3

Making Connections Economically

In Lesson 2, I didn't write about the wordy compound subordinating conjunction *in addition to the fact that* because I wanted to talk about it with the other *the-fact-that* compounds. Although it is the only subordinating conjunction of addition, I avoid it and use *and* or one of the conjunctive adverbs. Instead of writing, "In addition to the fact that I lost the game, I was injured." I write: "I lost the game and was injured." If I want to emphasize my injury, I might use *furthermore*: "I lost the game. Furthermore, I was injured."

For other *the-fact-that* subordinating conjunctions, there are shorter replacements. For *in contrast to the fact*, *in spite of the fact that*, and *despite the fact that*, I use *although*. For longer subordinating conjunctions of condition such as *in the event that*, *in case of the fact that*, *provided that* and *providing that,* I use *if*. The *that* could be dropped from *provided that* and *providing that*, but I still prefer *if*. For *as a result of the fact*, *due to the fact that*, and *owing to the fact that,* I use *because*. But I don't use *because* or the preposition *because of* in the same sentence with *the reason* or *the cause* as subjects in order to avoid a redundancy: "The reason I lost is because I served poorly," or "The cause for my loss was because of my poor serve." Instead I write, "The reason I lost is that I served poorly." Better would be, "I lost because I served poorly."

The subordinating conjunctions of motive *in order that* and *so that* have shorter, more formal versions with *that*: "That he might win more often, he practices." And there's a shorter more informal version of *so that*: "So I could win, I cheated." But I like the infinitive of reason, introduced by *in order to*: "In order to write more effectively, I studied English syntax." And *in order* could be omitted, "To write more effectively, I studied English syntax." Motive can be shown with just the preposition *for*, too. In "I went to town to buy milk" *for* can replace the infinitive phrase: "I went to town for milk."

The following exercises will have some connectives other than the ones discussed here, and the answers will show you some of the possibilities for saving words on your connectives.

Exercise 1

In the following sentences, strike through the redundant words or rewrite the sentence to avoid the extra words.

1. In addition to the fact that I wrote *Connecting For Coherence*, I wrote *Purposeful Punctuation*.

2. I lost the game in spite of the fact that I served well.

3. As a result of the fact that I got to school late, I missed the test.

4. In the event that we lose this match, we will be eliminated.

5. They left during the time that we were working.

6. I want Henry to comb his hair in addition to the fact that I want him to brush his teeth.

7. At the time that I was in San Marcos, no games were being played.

8. Despite the fact that he failed the exam, he passed the class.

Exercise 2

In the following sentences, strike through the redundant words or rewrite the sentence to avoid the extra words.

1. We were late for the exam owing to the fact that all of the buses were completely full.

2. In addition to the fact that he graduated with honors, he also was given a scholarship.

3. They both were going on to graduate school in spite of the fact that they had difficulty each and every semester during the course of their entire academic careers.

4. During the time that they were fellow classmates, they had made extensive future plans together.

5. As a result of having planned for their future, they were fully satisfied that they would progress forward to the final end of their course of studies successfully.

Lesson 4

What's Missing?

When most writers hear the word *ellipsis*, they think of the three dots used to indicate that something has been omitted from a quotation. But many grammatical elements are routinely omitted from English sentences with no dots to indicate it. Most allow us to save words, to keep from saying the same thing twice. A few are structure words. One frequently raising contention is the deletion of the *that* which introduces noun clauses. In a sentence such as "I know that he will be here soon," teachers emphasizing economy mark *that* out. But if a student has left it out, teachers emphasizing clarity often write it in. If the sentence is clear without it, I never correct it, leaving it to the writer's habit and choice. But with compounds and series of nominal clauses, the choice seems clearer. Some students write sentences with multiple noun clauses and leave out all of the *that*s: "I know Bob will be working, Joe will be doing homework, and Susan will be playing softball." In sentences like these I prefer all three *that*s: "I know that Bob will be working, that Joe will be doing homework, and that Susan will be playing softball." Teachers emphasizing economy may insist on only one *that*: "I know that Bob will be working, ~~that~~ Joe will be doing homework, and ~~that~~ Susan will be playing softball."

As problem I've found in student writing is a misplaced *that* or an excess one: "I know when I am reading in bed that I often go to sleep." The *that* should be before the *when*. Often student writers double up on the *that*s: "I know that when I am reading in bed ~~that~~ I often go to sleep."

When the subject and auxiliary verb of the *that* clauses are the same for each clause, the ellipsis is often more extensive. Instead of writing, "I know that Bill will enroll in college, that he will be successful. and that he will go on to a great career, I can write."I know that Bill will enroll in college, ~~that he will~~ be successful, and ~~that he will~~ go on to a great career." Similar to these nominal *that* clauses are clauses which complement certain predicate adjectives of confidence and doubt: "I am happy ~~that~~ I won the election," and "I am sure ~~that~~ he lost the election." Another similar *that* clause is the one which pairs with *so* to intensify an adjective or adverb: "He was so late ~~that~~ he missed the test," and "He ran so fast that he won the race." In each of these the *that* may be deleted. Again, being clear is more important than being economical. These clauses may be used in the same sentence: "I was so happy ~~that~~ I won the election ~~that~~ I threw a big party." I rarely omit these important connectives.

Another common ellipsis is in compound verb-modifying clauses. For example in short ones, the subsequent subordinating conjunctions are often omitted: "The baseball team lost because the shortstop made three throwing errors, ~~because~~ the relief pitcher walked four batters, and ~~because~~ the center fielder dropped two fly balls." If the sentence is long, I don't use this deletion because I know that the connectives help the reader understand the relationships in the sentence. Just as with the *that* clauses, the verb-modifying clauses often have more extensive ellipsis if there are common elements: "Bob lost because he double faulted often, ~~because he~~ missed the ball frequently on his backhand, and ~~because he~~ failed to return any of the lobs." Sometimes with long clauses, it is better to repeat the connectives to improve the cohesion.

Similar to the ellipsis with the *that* clauses is the first kind of ellipsis in relative clauses, those that modify nouns. This kind of ellipsis is called "object deletion" by transformational grammarians. When the relative word *whom*, *which*, or *that* functions as an object in the modifying clause, it may be omitted: "The house ~~which~~ I painted looks good," "The man ~~whom~~ I invited couldn't come," and "The tree ~~that~~ I removed was diseased." In these, I would not use the relative pronouns in my writing. But I would not remove them from writing I am editing. I may, if I wish, not use *when*, and *why*, the relative words used as adverbials in the modifying clause: "The time ~~when~~ I came was inappropriate," and "The reason ~~why~~ I came was inappropriate."

The second kind of ellipsis of noun-modifying clauses is called "relative deletion" by transformational grammarians. It is the simultaneous removal of one of the relative pronouns *who*, *which*, or *that* and one of the tense-marked *be* verbs *am, is, are, was,* or *were*. "The man ~~who is~~ cutting down the tree lives next door. "The house ~~which is~~ on the hill may fall," "The bond ~~which was~~ passed last year will cause my taxes to be higher," "My son's friend, ~~who is~~ a patent attorney, lives in Houston." I use these deletions unless I lose clarity by doing so.

Notice the ellipsis of the participle phrase ending my previous sentence. Writers don't like repeating whole verb phrases if we can help it. Notice here I used *doing it* instead of *doing so*. I also have *do* without the *so* or *it* to replace whole verb phrases: "She told me to wash the dishes carefully to avoid breaking them, so I washed the dishes carefully to avoid breaking them." Any of the three can allow me to avoid the repetition: "She told me to wash the dishes carefully to avoid breaking them, so I did it," "She told me to wash the dishes carefully to avoid breaking them, so I did so," "She told me to wash the dishes carefully to avoid breaking them, so I did."

There are two kinds of ellipses in verb-modifying clauses. In the first, the subject of the modifying clause and one of the *be* verbs is omitted if the subject of the modified clause and modifying clause are the same: "While ~~I was~~ cooking, I was listening to the radio." "Once ~~it is~~ completed, the assignment will be turned in immediately." I use this ellipsis frequently. But I am careful to have both subjects the same. Otherwise, I create the heinous error called faulty ellipsis: "While cooking, the radio is on," "Once completed, I will turn in the assignment." Neither the radio was cooking nor was I completed.

The second kind of ellipsis of verb modifying clauses is like the first, but there is an additional deletion of a *because*: "~~Because I was~~ sure that I would win, I toyed with my opponent." For this deletion, we have adjectives or verbs about knowing or not knowing. When it has a verb of knowing, the form of the verb is changed to the present participle. "Because I knew that I would win, I toyed with my opponent," becomes "Knowing that I would win, I toyed with my opponent." Here, too, I must be sure ~~that~~ the understood subject of the verb-modifying construction is the same as that of the main clause, or I have committed the sin writing teachers call the dangling modifier: "Sure ~~that~~ I would win, my opponent was toyed with," or "Knowing ~~that~~ I would win, my opponent was toyed with."

There are several other kinds of ellipsis, but none of them are as important to authors seeking economy as those above. One of the other kinds is the omission of the *by* prepositional phrase for agency with passive voice: "This book will be published in 2013." Another kind of ellipsis is that used to omit the expletive *there* and the *be* verb. "There will be a man here tomorrow to give flu shots" can be shortened to "A man will be here tomorrow to give flu shots."

Exercise 1

In the following sentences, strike through the redundant words or rewrite the sentence to avoid the extra words.

1. Bison, which were a primary form of sustenance for Indians, were slaughtered at will by Anglos.

2. Large gangs, which were composed of Mexican renegades and young Indian warriors from the Shawnee and Delaware tribes, were organized by ex-Anglo soldiers to hunt Apaches.

3. Like Huckleberry Finn, the "child" embarks on an escape to the west, which is reminiscent of the theme in the American masculine romance.

4. The people who were standing in line for tickets had been there for hours.

5. The man whom she married had lived next door since she was in elementary school.

6. The coaches believed that the students who were recruited to play football would graduate.

7. I know that Bob will finish first, that Joe will finish second, and that Bill will fail to finish.

8. Because Ruth worked late and because she didn't read her email, she didn't know that her husband had been delayed at his office and that he couldn't meet her.

9. I am confident that I will finish the ten kilometer race in record time.

10. I am so fit that I could run a marathon.

11. I am happy that Bob won the race, that Susan completed it, and that I placed third.

12. I know that the man who is cutting down the trees which are diseased is a workman who is competent.

13. There are some people who are working on the project already.

Exercise 2

The following sentences have clauses with faulty ellipsis or adjective or verb phrases with dangling modifiers. Change the main clause to eliminate the faultiness of the ellipsis or the dangling of the modifier. Add your own subjects as needed. Some may not have one of these faults.

1. While playing second base, three errors were made.

2. Confident that I would be accepted, space in the dormitory was reserved.

3. Once written, I must print the theme quickly.

4. Aware that I was being tested, great care was taken on each question.

5. Suspecting that I might be burglarized, bars were installed on my windows.

6. Not sure whether I had been accepted, I reapplied.

7. Irritated by the boy's behavior, a scolding was given him by his father.

8. Although tired, another game seemed like a good idea.

9. I heard that while sorting potatoes, many were thrown away because they were rotten.

Lesson 5

Staying Appropriate

Skinny writing is precise writing. It's writing that doesn't waste words, that stays on topic. With some kinds of writing, informal essays for example, it's not so important to be appropriate, but on others it is critical, particularly academic, legal, and technical writing.

If I am writing about how I am writing something or will write something, I am not writing on the subject. Should I stop here to tell my readers what my plan is for this lesson rather than launch into it, I am metawriting: "In this lesson I plan to cover the various ways writers may be off the subject and waste their readers' time on irrelevancies." The last part of that sentence is informative, but the first isn't. Obviously I have to plan, and you need to know what I will do in the lesson. But I can inform you with the lesson title and the thesis sentence.

Another kind of metawriting common in college themes is writing about how the reader of a work learns something or when. When writing about dramatic irony, I need to talk about when I learned something, or when writing about the author's exposition, I need to. But if I'm writing about when and how I learn about the work in question, I am wasting words, words I need to tell about the work. For example, commonly students write several sentences such as this: "In the very first scene we learn that Willy is despondent." Every report, every sentence, about a literary work could begin with when the reader learns about something, but to do so is to be off the subject.

Related to this is sentences such as "Throughout the entirety of the whole play, Colonel Kincaid is constantly taking about the horrors of trench warfare." *Constantly* and its partner, *always*, are overstatements and superfluous. The simple present and past tenses indicate continuing action. Prepositional phrases with *throughout* are sometimes needed particularly if after a certain part of the work, the situation or character changes. But they are commonly overused and unnecessary.

Similarly, I can write off the subject, by relating how confident or lacking in confidence I am. Most of the time when I'm writing something, I'm presenting my views about the topic. The reader should know that it's mine unless I say it's someone else's opinion. I shouldn't write: "~~In my own personal opinion, I think that~~ Colonel Kincaid is suffering trauma from his experience in the trenches during World War I. " And "my ~~own~~" is redundant no matter what it is used before. In the previous sentence I was wise to avoid "my ~~own~~ views." If I use *I believe, I think, I suppose,* or *I figure,* how sure can the reader be of how confident I am about what follows. If I just make an assertion without these, the reader will still suppose that the assertions are mine. Similarly, *seems* is usually unnecessary. Some students writers are fearful of making an assertion and place *seems* or *tends to* before each one. However, at times, writers do need to report how sure or unsure of their premises they are. Judgment is necessary in deciding when and how often to qualify. If I write, " ~~It is quite possible that~~ Colonel Kincaid is suffering trauma from his experience in the trenches during World War I," I have been wordily superfluous. If I am not sure, an occasional *possibly* is in order. But using too many leads to a loss of persuasive force.

I can also waste words by using wind-up words like *begins to* or *starts to,* "When they finally ~~begin to~~ tell this part of the family story, their daughter objects."

The word *actually* is inappropriate unless paired with *figuratively*, Heaberlin ~~actually~~ wrote a book about wasting words." *Surprisingly* would be a better word to suggest upsetting of expectations. This use of *actually* is quite common in speech, but *actually* is ~~actually~~ to be avoided in writing. Another superfluous word most of the time is *truly*. I've seldom seen a need for it, and I delete it when I am editing: "*Truly* is ~~truly~~ useless. I often find some uses of *very* unnecessary: "From the ~~very~~ first chapter, the protagonist is drunk" and "He was very rude."

Another common problem of many writers is failing to notice when they have said the same thing in consecutive clauses or phrases: "I stayed away from home ~~and didn't go back~~ for a long time."

Exercise 1

In the following sentences, strike through the redundant words or rewrite the sentence to avoid the extra words.

1. We learn in the first scene that the Miller gang wants to kill Will Kane.

2. I plan to tell you to avoid redundancies.

3. Among them as I mentioned previously was the Glanton gang,

4. From study of its gases we will learn how the planet was actually formed.

5. In my own personal opinion I think Harvey Pell was afraid of the Millers.

6. He was tracked by the very forces of the very governments that once hired them.

7. Her face is never truly fully illuminated by heavy lighting.

8. She doesn't want to show her true age.

9. Leonard is shown to very literally have died.

10. Mac will relapse back into alcohol.

11. He immediately begins to draw each item in his "leather ledgerbook."

Exercise 2

In the following sentences, strike through the redundant words or rewrite the sentence to avoid the extra words.

1. Pulp western novels and magazines contributed to the embellished perception of the mythic West, further enhanced by the Wild West shows of Buffalo Bill.

2. In one of the very few interviews Cormac McCarthy has given, he actually says "I've always been interested in the Southwest."

3. Her blue notebook seems to truly becomes the record of her actual emotions.

4. From the very beginning of the very first scene, the main protagonist is actually drunk.

5. I am absolutely positive that Kane and Cisco couldn't have won in a gunfight with so many gunmen.

6. You should write in your own words what you think about the movie *High Noon*.

7. Although these interpretations seem accurate, I offer a different interpretation and argue that the "evening redness in the west" evokes the symbolic image of a "bloodred" sun fading beyond the horizon.

Lesson 6

Using the Right Word

Gustave Flaubert, nineteenth-century French author of *Madame Bovary*, often spent a week writing a page of a novel. He was obsessive about finding *le mot juste*, translated as the *exact word* or *right word*. It's admirable to care so much about writing well. But most of us do not have the time or energy to write so carefully and precisely. And is it necessary? Some writing is just not that important. The effort needs to fit the importance of the writing. When writing an email to a student, though careful, I am not so careful as I am in writing a lesson in this style guide. Too much concern for precision in a first draft can sometimes end with a writer blocked and unable to finish an assignment. Too little concern can end with flabby, disorganized, imprecise prose. We must find a middle ground, fitting our effort to the importance of our document.

If we know our readers and subject well, we will feel less stress as we write and write more fluently and succinctly. But often we must select our words with more precision because we don't know what our readers know about the subject, what words they will understand. If I am writing about woodworking, will the readers know words such as *kerf, dado, miter*, or *bevel*. Can I use them? Or do I have to explain each as I write. Knowing when and when not to use technical terms is not the primary difficulty we have in choosing our words. Often the right word is an ordinary one, one we can find if we search with a smidgen of the effort of a writer such as Flaubert. I could write, "I am going to see the doctor to talk to him about my problem in dealing with my swollen knee. "But with a little thought I will realize the every-day word *consult* is the word I need, "I will consult the doctor about my swollen knee."

I can write with inappropriate words, called malapropisms. If I use an incorrect word for a word with a similar sound, I've said something which will often make people laugh. Shakespeare's character Dogberry made such errors, but Richard Brinsley Sheridan made them famous with his character Mrs. Malaprop in his play *The Rivals* (1775). She used *illiterate* for *obliterate*, *allegory* for *alligator*, and *reprehend* for *apprehend*. One of my students once wrote: "I seized working at Walmart."

Most of the writers I admire, those who write concise, informative prose, say that they edit, edit, edit. What most of them do is look carefully at each sentence, seeking a clearer more precise phrasing, seeking *le mot juste*.

Exercise 1
Edit the following sentences by finding a more precise word in order to save words.

1. I asked Jim to give me some suggestions about what I should do in order to get a job.

2. I need to look for information about what went on at the battle of the Alamo.

3. I've been told that the illness of children which causes your lower face to swell up and hurt is more severe in adults.

4. I will get completely rid of the errors I've been making in my writing.

5. The negative things people have been saying about me are not how I want to be seen.

Exercise 2
In the following sentences, strike through the redundant words or rewrite the sentence to avoid the extra words.

1. The character bounced back and forth between her own diluted reality and her own guilt.

2. The woman lives in her own reality because she does not like the world she currently lives in.

3. Blanche has room for redemption whereas Stanley proves to be completely irredeemable.

4. When he finally does make a genuine choice, he comes to know a freedom which he previously had not even known existed.

5 As the scene goes on, Hickey then takes off his suit jacket, and he starts to look just as scruffy and underdressed as the rest of the men.

6. My opinion could be biased due to that fact that I am used to seeing Alec Baldwin play more comedic roles, and I am not used to seeing him in more serious roles.

7. The entire first half of *High Noon* has left Kane and the audience waiting for the arrival of Frank Miller.

8. The viewers watching the movie *High Noon* soon learn about the Quaker religion that Amy has chosen to have.

9. The use of time is also used to form suspense.

10. *High Noon* is one of my favorites of the older Westerns we have seen so far.

11. He stares out the window and sings the exact song she had mentioned.

12. The cast is practically a laundry list of the standard characters found in almost every great story ever told.

13. He magnifies facial expressions to bring insight to the inner thoughts of each character.

14. The characters each bring their own past to the stagecoach in a unique way.

15. Doc Boone adds a comedic relief to the story because of his over exaggerated drunkenness and silly behavior.

16.They were added for entertainment purposes but did not contribute to the narrative at all.

17. This story has the potential and capabilities to take place anywhere in the world, which brings the assumption that the Southwestern aspects were included for comedic purposes.

18. She is comedic in nature because of her stereotypical housewife attire and exaggerated facial expressions.

19. Although the title itself is *True Grit*, the older version of this story does not appear to be "gritty" enough for the plot.

20. While watching the 1983 film *The Ballad of Gregorio Cortez*, I noticed that I truly enjoyed this film.

21. Despite the discussion we had in class, I thought the lighting Young used gave the film a natural documentary feel to it.

22. During his chase/fight scene with H.I. and Ed, the music played throughout and made Small seem even more menacing than before.

23. The audience is clueless to the amount of distance between the Rangers and Cortez.

24. After watching *No Country for Old Men*, I have to say that I now have extreme respect for the Coen brothers.

25 He completely deserved the academy award that he received for his role in the movie, *No Country for Old Men*.

26. His lack of remorse attributes to his scary demeanor.

27. He says few words and maintains a blank stare in his eyes.

28. They hastily return while duplicating the same dramatic scream.

29. The two accidents cannot be equally compared.

30. He wears a hot grey trench coat and a grey fedora hat.

31. I must make quarrel with regards to the scene where Cortez is being chased by the posse of marshals and mercenaries right next to the train in an open field.

32. The movie is actually about a couple that is composed of an ex-convict who has held up many corner stores in the past and the female cop who took his mug shot every time he went to prison.

33. I would first of all like to start off by analyzing Chigurh as I did with my assigned group.

34. Mac ends up getting knocked out cold in his drunken stupor.

35. The two end up falling in love.

36. The Coen Brothers used various overhead or birds-eye-view shots to capture the entirety of a scene in the barren desert.

37. They also used plenty of shots that were low to the ground to capture specific points of view.

38. He still remains loyal to the town.

39. Nothing could hinder him in his attempt to win over Dallas at all costs.

40. The love Ringo contained for her completely dissolved any doubt in his mind.

41. These techniques combined were sure to make for an excellent and successful film.

42. The unusual nature of the weapon choice went along with the other bizarre traits Chigurh possessed.

43. We got stuck with some unnecessary scenes that could have been cut shorter or even cut completely out.

Appendix

Answers to Exercises with Comments

Lesson 1

Exercise 1

1. The wine glass is ~~completely~~ empty.

2. Pam's dress is the ~~exact~~ same as Lynn's.

3. That is an ~~extremely~~ unique expression of distaste.

4. It is ~~absolutely~~ essential that he buy this book.

5. The fire ants ~~completely~~ annihilated our quail.

6. Carol has ~~consciously~~ chosen to omit this part of the story from the family history.

7. It was marred by the ~~brutal~~ violence of Manifest Destiny.

8. Anglos ~~completely~~ demolished the fort and set fire to the church.

9. Following ~~the conclusion of~~ the Mexican-American War in 1848, Mexico ceded control of California and New Mexico to the United States in 1849.

10. In *Stagecoach*, the deviations from Ernest Haycox's "The Stage to Lordsburg" were relatively small ~~in scale~~.

11. Unlike the virtuous frontier hero, McCarthy's "child" is the ~~complete~~ opposite.

12. We made ~~advanced~~ reservation for dinner.

13. He is working on the ~~basic~~ fundamentals of tennis.

14. I blended ~~together~~ a peach and a plum.

15. For a brief moment I gave it careful scrutiny.

I looked at it briefly but carefully.

16. We collaborated ~~together~~ in order to classify the insects ~~into groups.~~

17. Fred and I competed ~~with each other~~ until the ~~final~~ end of the match.

18. We saw ~~with our own eyes~~ how he was behaving.

19. Fred Thompson was extradited ~~back~~ last week.

20. The product was introduced ~~for the first time~~ on television at the Super Bowl ~~football~~ game.

21. I liked McCarthy's ~~fiction~~ novel *The Crossing*.

22. There has not ~~yet~~ been an announcement from the Provost's office.

23. He wrote an autobiography ~~of his own life~~.

24. His home run gave the Bobcats a 3-2 lead, which they never relinquished ~~the rest of the way~~.

25. The Owls lost their last game, a series ender against Tulane, but won four of their previous five ~~before that~~.

26. The Rangers' game with the Diamondbacks was postponed ~~to a later date~~.

27. When he raised his voice ~~to a higher level~~, it wasn't as clear.

28. He equates the two ~~together~~.

29. I could just hear my sister saying the exact same things as Jen did in Act I.

My sister said the same things as Jen in Act I.

Lesson 2

Exercise 1

1. His sense of self is discontinuous with the identity he has created in the rest of the family narrative, ~~and~~ so he has chosen not to tell the story until this moment.

2. It encouraged this sense of optimism as well as the demand for more territory.

It encouraged this sense of optimism and the demand for more territory.

3. He was tired not only of reading essays but also of writing themes.

He was tired of reading essays and writing themes.

4. Not only was he arrested, but he was additionally sent to prison, too.

He was arrested and sent to prison.

5. Bill with his friend is going to be able to work during the holidays.

Bill and his friend can work during the holidays.

6. Tom and Bill ~~both~~ wanted to go to a college in the Southwest.

7. The pilgrims ~~all~~ suffered during that first winter.

8. Bill lost most of his money gambling. And ~~what's more~~ he had no way to get home.

9. Guy along with Ralph is leaving for Boston soon.

Guy and Ralph are leaving for Boston soon.

10. He ate three pieces of pie and some ice cream ~~as well.~~

Exercise 2

1. Not only was Bill completely lost, but Gilbert was, too.

Bill and Gilbert were lost.

2. And ~~moreover, both~~ their stories were incredible ~~to believe~~.

3. They all joined together for a joint collaboration.

They collaborated.

4. They ~~both~~ knelt ~~down~~ to be knighted.

5. Their ~~past~~ history was ~~completely~~ full of ~~bad~~ misbehavior ~~as well~~.

They had misbehaved frequently.

6. They ~~all~~ will meet ~~with each other~~ to discuss a ~~major~~ breakthrough.

7. Not only have they together been responsible for new innovations but also for new inventions as well.

They have been responsible for innovations and inventions.

8. Not only were they all proud of what they had originally created, but they also over exaggerated its importance.

They were proud of their creation and exaggerated its importance.

9. My past experience along with my past record shows how I have completely eliminated my bad misdeeds.

My experience and my record show how I have eliminated my misdeeds.

10. He couldn't possibly descend down into the depths of sad depressive feelings without joining together with his friends to discuss his problem.

He couldn't descend into depression without meeting his friends to discuss his problem.

11. Additionally, the second half of this film also seems to drag on and on forever with scenes that do nothing to propel the storyline forward.

The second half of this film drags on and on with scenes doing nothing to help the story.

Lesson 3

Exercise 1

1. In addition to the fact that I wrote *Connecting For Coherence*, I wrote *Purposeful Punctuation*.

I wrote *Connecting For Coherence* and *Purposeful Punctuation*.

2. I lost the game in spite of the fact that I served well.

These are some of the ways to show contrast.

I lost the game although I served well.

I lost the game in spite of serving well.

I served well, but I lost the game.

I served well. However, I lost the game.

I served well. I lost the game, though.

3. As a result of the fact that I got to school late, I missed the test.

These are some of the better ways to show cause.

Because I got to school late, I missed the test.

Because of getting to school late, I missed the test.

I got to school late, so I missed the test.

I got to school late. Therefore, I missed the test.

4. In the event that we lose this match, we will be eliminated.

These are some of the better ways to show condition.

If we lose this match, we will be eliminated.

Unless we win this match, we will be eliminated.

We must win this match. Otherwise, we will be eliminated

5. They left during the time that we were working.

They left while we were working.

6. I want Henry to comb his hair in addition to the fact that I want him to brush his teeth.

I want Henry to comb his hair and brush his teeth.

7. At the time that I was in San Marcos, no games were being played.

When I was in San Marcos, no games were being played.

While I was in San Marcos, no games were being played.

8. Despite the fact that he failed the exam, he passed the class.

Here are two of the better ways to show contrast.

He failed the exam, yet he passed the class.

Although he failed the exam, he passed the class.

Exercise 2

1. We were late for the exam owing to the fact that all of the buses were completely full.

We were late for the exam because the buses were full.

2. In addition to the fact that he graduated with honors, he also was given a scholarship.

He graduated with honors and was given a scholarship.

3. They both were going on to graduate school in spite of the fact that they had difficulty each and every semester during the course of their entire academic careers.

They were going to graduate school although they had difficulty every semester.

4. During the time that they were fellow classmates, they had made extensive future plans together.

While they were classmates, they had made extensive plans.

5. As a result of having planned for their future, they were fully satisfied that they would progress forward to the final end of their course of studies successfully.

Because of their planning, they were satisfied that they would complete their studies.

Lesson 4

Exercise 1

1. Bison, ~~which were~~ a primary form of sustenance for Indians, were slaughtered at will by Anglos.

2. Large gangs, ~~which were~~ composed of Mexican renegades and young Indian warriors from the Shawnee and Delaware tribes, were organized by ex-Anglo soldiers to hunt Apaches.

3. Like Huckleberry Finn, the "child" embarks on an escape to the west, which is reminiscent of the theme in the American masculine romance.

This *which* clause is modifying the verb phrase which precedes, not a noun, so deleting the *which is* could cause a problem in understanding. I didn't change it.

4. The people ~~who were~~ standing in line for tickets had been there for hours.

5. The man ~~whom~~ she married had lived next door since she was in elementary school.

I seldom write *whom*. If I weren't deleting *whom* I would use *that* for it. I only use *whom* in the most formal writing.

6. The coaches believed that the students ~~who were~~ recruited to play football would graduate.

7. I know that Bob will finish first, that Joe will finish second, and that Bill will fail to finish.

There are three possibilities here. The one showing the structure most clearly is the one above. There are two other possibilities.

I know that Bob will finish first, Joe will finish second, and Bill will fail to finish.

I know Bob will finish first, Joe will finish second, and Bill will fail to finish.

I like the one with one *that* the best.

8. Because Ruth worked late and ~~because she~~ didn't read her email, she didn't know that her husband had been delayed at his office and that he couldn't meet her.

Leaving the second *because* would be fine and probably preferred if the first clause were longer. Keeping the second *that* shows the structure more clearly.

9. I am confident ~~that~~ I will finish the ten kilometer race in record time.

10. I am so fit ~~that~~ I could run a marathon.

11. I am happy that Bob won the race, ~~that~~ Susan completed it, and ~~that~~ I placed third.

The comment for #7 applies here.

12. I know that the man who is cutting down the trees which are diseased is a workman who is competent.

I know that the man cutting down the diseased trees is a competent workman.

If I drop the *that*, I can cause a temporary misreading.

13. There are some people who are working on the project already.

Some people are working on the project already.

Exercise 2

1. While playing second base, three errors were made.

While playing second base, I made three errors.

2. Confident that I would be accepted, space in the dormitory was reserved.

Confident that I would be accepted, I reserved space in the dormitory.

3. Once written, I must print the theme quickly.

Once written, the theme must be printed quickly.

4. Aware that I was being tested, great care was taken on each question.

Aware that I was being tested, I took great care on each question.

5. Suspecting that I might be burglarized, bars were installed on my windows.

Suspecting that I might be burglarized, I installed bars on my windows.

6. Not sure whether I had been accepted, I reapplied.

This is correct.

7. Irritated by the boy's behavior, a scolding was given him by his father.

 Irritated by the boy's behavior, his father scolded him.

8. Although tired, another game seemed like a good idea.

 Although tired, I thought another game seemed like a good idea.

9. I heard that while sorting potatoes, many were thrown away because they were rotten.

I heard that while sorting potatoes, they threw many away because they were rotten.

Lesson 5

Exercise 1

1. ~~We learn in the first scene that~~ the Miller gang wants to kill Will Kane.

2. I plan to tell you to avoid redundancies.

You should avoid redundancies.

3. Among them ~~as I mentioned previously~~ was the Glanton gang,

4. From study of its gases we know how the planet was ~~actually~~ formed.

5. ~~In my own personal opinion I think~~ Harvey Pell was afraid of the Millers.

6. He was tracked by the ~~very~~ forces of the ~~very~~ governments that once hired them.

7. Her face is never ~~truly~~ fully illuminated ~~by heavy lighting~~.

8. She doesn't want to show her ~~true~~ age.

9. Leonard is shown to very literally have died.

Leonard is shown dead.

10. Mac will relapse back into alcohol.

Mac will go back to drinking.

11. He immediately begins to draw each item in his "leather ledgerbook."

He immediately draws each item in his "leather ledgerbook."

Exercise 2

1. Pulp western novels and magazines contributed to the embellished perception of the mythic West, ~~further~~ enhanced by the Wild West shows of Buffalo Bill.

2. In one of the very few interviews Cormac McCarthy has given, he actually says "I've always been interested in the Southwest."

In one of the few interviews with Cormac McCarthy, he says "I've always been interested in the Southwest."

3. Her blue notebook ~~seems to truly~~ becomes the record of her ~~actual~~ emotions.

4. From the ~~very beginning of the very~~ first scene, the ~~main~~ protagonist is ~~actually~~ drunk.

5. ~~I am absolutely positive that~~ Kane and Cisco couldn't have won in a gunfight against so many gunmen.

6. You should write in your own words what you think about the movie *High Noon*.

You should write about *High Noon*.

7. Although these interpretations seem accurate, I offer a different interpretation and argue that the "evening redness in the west" evokes the symbolic image of a "bloodred" sun fading beyond the horizon.

The "evening redness in the west" evokes the symbolic image of a "bloodred" sun fading below the horizon.

Lesson 6

Exercise 1

1. I asked Jim to give me some suggestions about what I should do in order to get a job.

I asked Jim for advice about getting a job.

2. I need to look for information about what went on at the battle of the Alamo.

I need to research the battle of the Alamo.

3. I've been told that the illness of children which causes your lower face to swell up and hurt is more severe in adults.

I heard that mumps is more severe for adults than children.

4. I will get completely rid of the errors I've been making in my writing.

I will eliminate my writing errors.

5. The negative things people have been saying about me are not how I want to be seen.

Exercise 2

1. The character bounced back and forth between her own diluted reality and her own guilt.

Diluted is malaprop. The writer meant to say *deluded*.

The character bounced between her delusion and her guilt.

2. The woman lives in her own reality because she does not like the world she currently lives in.

The woman constructs her reality because she does not like her real world.

3. Blanche has room for redemption whereas Stanley proves to be completely irredeemable.

Blanche can be redeemed, but Stanley can't.

4. When he finally does make a genuine choice, he comes to know a freedom which he previously had not even known existed.

When he finally chooses, he finds an unknown freedom.

5. As the scene goes on, Hickey then takes off his suit jacket and he starts to look just as scruffy and underdressed as the rest of the men.

When Hickey takes off his suit jacket, he looks as scruffy and underdressed as the others.

6. My opinion could be biased due to that fact that I am used to seeing Alec Baldwin play more comedic roles, and I am not used to seeing him in more serious roles.

I may be biased because I am used to seeing Alec Baldwin play comedic roles, not serious ones.

7. The entire first half of *High Noon* has left Kane and the audience waiting for the arrival of Frank Miller.

In the first half of *High Noon*, Kane waits for Frank Miller to arrive.

8. The viewers watching the movie *High Noon* soon learn about the Quaker religion that Amy has chosen to have.

Amy is a Quaker.

9. The use of time is also used to form suspense.

Time adds to the suspense.

10. *High Noon* is one of my favorites of the older Westerns we have seen so far.

***High Noon* is one of my favorite older Westerns.**

11. Mac stares out the window and sings the ~~exact~~ song she had mentioned.

12. The cast is ~~practically~~ a laundry list of the ~~standard~~ characters ~~found~~ in almost every great story ~~ever told~~.

13. He magnifies facial expressions to bring insight to the inner thoughts of each character.

He uses close ups to show what each character thinks.

14. The characters ~~each~~ bring their ~~own~~ past to the stagecoach in a unique way.

This is shorter, but still isn't much better.

15. Doc Boone adds a comedic relief to the story because of his over exaggerated drunkenness and silly behavior.

Doc Boone adds humor by his exaggerated drunkenness and silliness.

16. They were added for entertainment purposes but did not contribute to the narrative at al.

They were added to entertain but did not contribute to the narrative.

17. This story has the potential and capabilities to take place anywhere in the world, which brings the assumption that the Southwestern aspects were included for comedic purposes.

This story could have been set anywhere in the world, so the Southwestern scenes were included for comedic purposes.

18. She is comedic in nature because of her stereotypical housewife attire and exaggerated facial expressions.

She is funny because of her stereotypical housewife attire and exaggerated facial expressions.

19. Although the title ~~itself~~ is *True Grit*, the older version ~~of this story~~ does not appear to be "gritty" enough ~~for the plot~~.

20. While watching the 1983 film *The Ballad of Gregorio Cortez*, I noticed that I truly enjoyed this film.

I liked *The Ballad of Gregorio Cortez*.

21. Despite the discussion we had in class, I thought the lighting Young used gave the film a natural documentary feel to it.

Young's lighting made the film feel like a documentary.

22. During his chase/fight scene with H.I. and Ed, the music played throughout and made Small seem even more menacing than before.

During the chase scene with H.I. and Ed, the music played continuously and made Small seem even more menacing.

23. The audience is clueless to the ~~amount of~~ distance between the Rangers and Cortez.

24. After watching *No Country for Old Men*, I have to say that I now have extreme respect for the Coen brothers.

I now have great respect for the Coen brothers because of *No Country for Old Men*.

25 He completely deserved the academy award that he received for his role in the movie, *No Country for Old Men*.

He deserved his academy award for *No Country for Old Men*.

26. His lack of remorse attributes to his scary demeanor.

Attributes is a good example of a malapropism.

His remorselessness contributes to his scariness.

27. He says few words and maintains a blank stare ~~in his eyes~~.

28. They hastily return while duplicating the ~~same~~ dramatic scream.

29.The two accidents cannot be ~~equally~~ compared.

30. He wears a hot grey trench coat and a grey fedora ~~hat~~.

 31.~~I must make quarrel with regards to the scene where~~ Cortez is being chased by the posse of marshals and mercenaries ~~right~~ next to the train in an open field.

What the quarrel is is not clear.

32. The movie is actually about a couple that is composed of an ex-convict who has held up many corner stores and the female cop who took his mug shot every time he went to prison.

The movie is about an ex-convict who has has held up corner stores and the female cop who took his mug shot when he went to prison.

33. I would first of all like to start off by analyzing Chigurh as I did with my assigned group.

None of this is informative.

34. Mac ends up getting knocked out cold in his drunken stupor.

Mac gets knocked out because he was drunk.

35. The two end up falling in love.

They fall in love.

36. The Coen Brothers used various overhead or birds-eye-view shots to capture the entirety of a scene in the barren desert.

The Coen Brothers shot from the birds-eye-view to capture the whole scene in the barren desert.

37. They also used plenty of shots that were low to the ground to capture specific points of view.

They frequently shot close to the ground to capture unusual perspectives.

38. He ~~still~~ remains loyal to the town.

39. Nothing could hinder him in his attempt to win over Dallas ~~at all costs.~~

40. The love Ringo contained for her completely dissolved any doubt in his mind.

Ringo love for her prevented any doubts.

41. These techniques combined were sure to make for an excellent and successful film.

These techniques would make the film excellent and successful.

42. The unusual nature of the weapon choice went along with the other bizarre traits Chigurh possessed.

The unusual choice of weapons fit the other bizarre traits of Chigurh.

43. We got stuck with some unnecessary scenes that could have been cut shorter or even cut completely out.

Some scenes could have been shortened or cut out.

www.ingramcontent.com/pod-product-compliance
Lightning Source LLC
LaVergne TN
LVHW061302060426
835509LV00016B/1683